The Library of
NATIVE AMERICANS

The Kiowa
of Texas

Lucile Davis

The Rosen Publishing Group's
PowerKids Press™
New York

For my dad, George J. Davis, 2/5/14 to 11/25/01

The editors wish to than Paul Calcaterra for his expertise.

Published in 2003 by The Rosen Publishing Group, Inc.
29 East 21st Street, New York, NY 10010

Photo and Illustration Credits: Cover and pp. 12, 17, 21, 24, 27 courtesy National Museum of the American Indian, Smithsonian Institution (cover, T021670, photo by Pam Dewey; p. 12, S123238, photo by Pam Dewey; p. 17, S213388, photo by Carmelo Guadagno; p. 21, N30953, photo by Carmelo Guadagno; p. 24, N28597, photo by Carmelo Guadagno; p. 27, S036493, photo by Janine Jones); p. 4 Erica Clendening; p. 6 © George D. Lepp/CORBIS; pp. 9, 34 © CORBIS; pp. 11, 18, 31, 44 courtesy Western History/Genealogy Department, Denver Public Library; pp. 14, 19, 22, 36, 41, 48 courtesy of Paul Calcaterra; p. 33 © Bill Ross/CORBIS; p. 39 © David Muench/CORBIS; p. 43 © Bettmann/CORBIS; p. 47 © Danny Lehman/CORBIS; p. 50 © Lindsay Hebberd/CORBIS; p. 52 courtesy Western History Collections, University of Oklahoma Libraries; p. 55 © Roger Ressmeyer/CORBIS.

Book Design: Erica Clendening

Davis, Lucile.
      The Kiowa of Texas / Lucile Davis.
          p. cm. — (The library of Native Americans)
      Includes bibliographical references and index.
      Contents: An introduction to the Kiowa—Kiowa on the plains—Other features of Kiowa life—Contact and conflict—Adapting and thriving.
      ISBN 0-8239-6434-5
      1. Kiowa Indians—History—Juvenile literature 2. Kiowa Indians—Social life and customs—Juvenile literature. [1. Kiowa Indians. 2. Indians of North America—Texas.] I. Title. II. Series.
E99.K5 D39 2002
978.004'9749—dc21

                                                2002003786

Manufactured in the United States of America

Contents

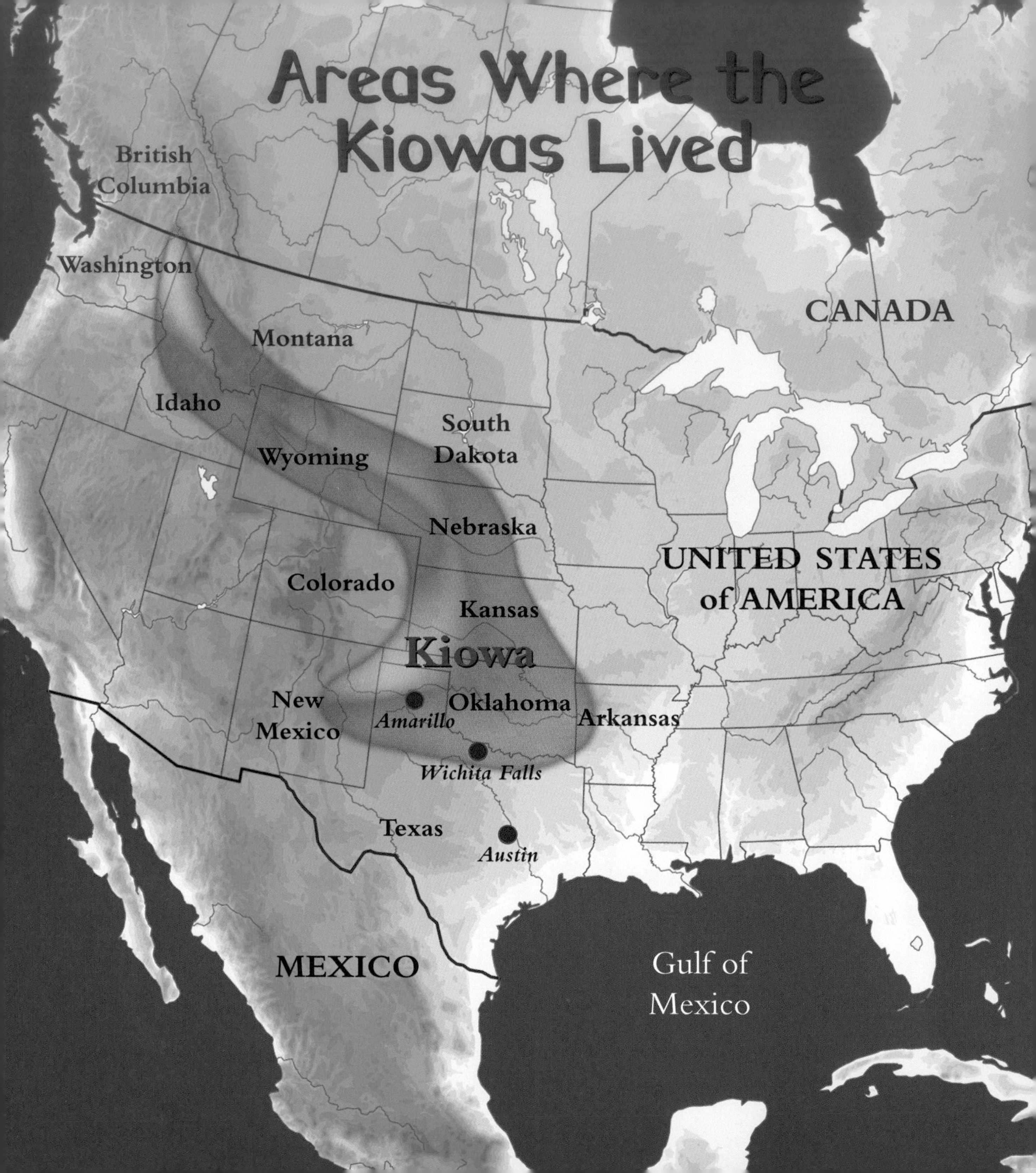

Areas Where the Kiowas Lived

British Columbia

Washington

CANADA

Montana

Idaho

Wyoming

South Dakota

Nebraska

UNITED STATES of AMERICA

Colorado

Kansas

Kiowa

New Mexico

Oklahoma

Amarillo

Arkansas

Wichita Falls

Texas

Austin

MEXICO

Gulf of Mexico

One

An Introduction to the Kiowa

The Kiowas are a Native American group who played a major role in Texas and U.S. history. Kiowas were nomads, people who wandered instead of living in one place. They followed the animals that they hunted for food and clothing. Their travels took them from the northwestern mountains of present-day western Montana to the southern Great Plains of North America, in present-day Oklahoma, Texas, and New Mexico. The Kiowas arrived on the southern Great Plains sometime between 1775 and 1790.

They were living on the Great Plains in the 1800s as the settlers from the United States began to move west in search of land. The Kiowas needed open land where they were free to wander. The settlers were also looking for land. However, unlike the Kiowa, the settlers wanted to own the land. This put the Kiowas and the settlers in conflict. This conflict turned into a bloody war, much of which was fought in Texas. This conflict would cast the Kiowas as "spoilers" in Texas and U.S. history. A spoiler is one whose actions ruin someone else's plans. Being a spoiler was not part of the Kiowas' plans. They wanted to preserve their way of life and to defend their territory.

This map highlights the areas in which the Kiowas lived. Originally from British Columbia and western Montana, the Kiowas traveled south to the southern Great Plains.

Before the conflict with settlers, the Kiowa held the territory from Oklahoma to New Mexico. After the conflict, they settled in and around Fort Sill, Anadarko, and Apache, Oklahoma. Eventually they were able to gain rights as citizens of the United States and to reclaim many of their traditions. Today, the Kiowa call themselves *Koi-gwu*. It is thought the name stands for two halves of the body or face, each half looking different. Kiowa is the current English language spelling of the name.

Origins of the Kiowa

The early days of the Kiowa are not known. Scholars say the ancient ancestors of the Kiowa crossed from Siberia over the frozen tundra to Alaska. Tribal memory places the Kiowas in the territory of

As the Kiowas traveled south, they encountered geysers such as this one in present-day Yellowstone National Park.

western Montana. Anthropologists believe that the Kiowa came from a mountainous region in what is now southeast British Columbia. The earliest known Kiowa hunting grounds were between the headwaters of the Yellowstone and Missouri Rivers. The Kiowas hunted on foot and used dogs to carry their belongings. As the Kiowas hunted, they traveled south.

After a time, the Kiowas found a place where geysers shot boiling water high out of the ground. The place is now known as Yellowstone National Park in Montana. The Kiowa hunted in the cold mountains that rose up around the geysers. They named the mountains *Koi-Kope*, "Mountains of the Kiowa." We know them as the Rocky Mountains.

While living in this area, they met a band now known as the Kiowa-Apaches. Neither Kiowa nor Apache, the Kiowa-Apaches were a band of Athapaskans distantly

Creation Myth

Kiowas tell of a time when the world was dark. Saynday, a supernatural being, called them into the world. He tapped on a hollow cottonwood tree and pulled the Kiowa through an owl hole one at a time. Many people were under ground, and they all did not get out. A woman whose body was swollen with child got stuck in the log. No more people got through. Those who did called themselves Kwu-da, "going out." They also called themselves Tepda, meaning "going out" or "coming out."

related to the Sarsis. Although they are considered a part of the Kiowa movement, their language is different than the Kiowas'. The Kiowas spoke a language thought to be an offshoot of the Azteco-Tanoan group. The small band of people now known as the Kiowa-Apache joined and became a part of the Kiowa.

The Kiowas were neighbors of the Flathead Indians. Native Americans from the Pacific Northwest also came to trade shells for animal skins. Life was good and hunting brought the Kiowas everything that they needed.

A dispute between two Kiowa chiefs resulted in a split in the tribe. The chief who lost the conflict withdrew his group and traveled north. They were never heard from again. They came to be known as *A-az-tan-hap*, or "those who went away suspiciously." The leader of the winning group took his people southeast. There they met the Crows. This meeting was a life-changing experience.

Life Changes

The journey from the northeast was slow for the Kiowas. They traveled on foot. The only pack animals the Kiowas had were dogs. The dogs dragged bundles tied to travois (TRAH-vwah). A travois was two long poles connected at one end by a net or platform. Bundles containing their belongings were strapped on the net or platform. The other ends of the poles were tied to a harness worn by the dog.

A dog could drag from 35 to 75 pounds (16–34 kg) on a travois, depending on the size and health of the dog.

Hunting before the Kiowas had horses was a difficult process. In the time before horses, hunting often was a group effort. A few hunters

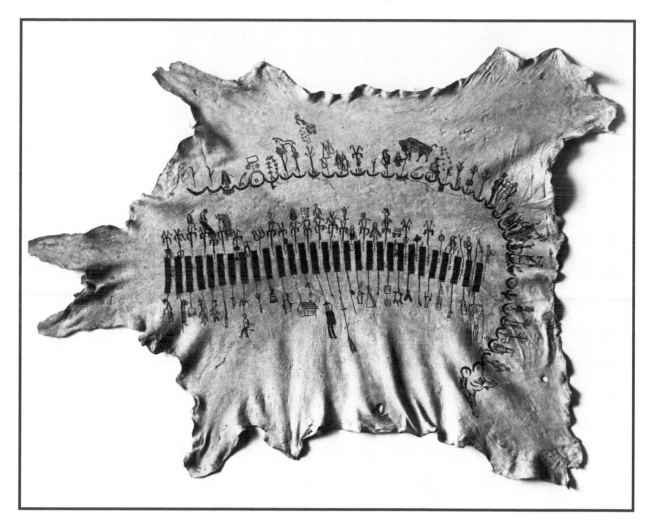

This Kiowa calendar was painted on animal skin.

would go upwind and chase the animals into a brush corral. If a cliff or closed canyon was nearby, they drove the deer, antelope, or buffalo over the cliff or into the canyon, killing as many as possible. By hunting in this manner, the Kiowas could secure enough meat for all. After the kill, the Kiowa men would stay in the area until the women processed the meat and skins and packed them for traveling.

Meeting the Crows

The Kiowas made their way across the Yellowstone River. Just east of the river lived the Crows. The two tribes became friends. The Kiowas took up hunting in the Black Hills. This area is in present-day southeast Montana and northeast Wyoming.

The Kiowa way of hunting changed when they met the Crows in 1700. The Crows had horses and taught the Kiowas how to ride. Smart, and able to adapt to new ways quickly, the Kiowas became expert horsemen, horse traders, and horse breeders.

Spanish explorers had brought horses to the North American continent in the 1500s. Indian contact with the Spaniards brought horses into use on the southern plains of the continent. This created a new way of life for the Plains Indians, bringing changes in hunting and traveling.

The Crows acquired horses through trade with Indians from the southern plains. The Crows were farmers. They used horses to hunt game. The Kiowas used horses to hunt buffalo. They came to depend on buffalo for everything that they needed. Indians on horse-back could ride along side a stampeding herd of buffalo and kill the animals with a bow and arrow or with rifles later obtained from Europeans. The women would ride out to the killing field to skin the

This photo shows Kiowa men on horseback. When the Kiowas acquired horses, their way of life changed. They came to depend on horses for hunting and traveling.

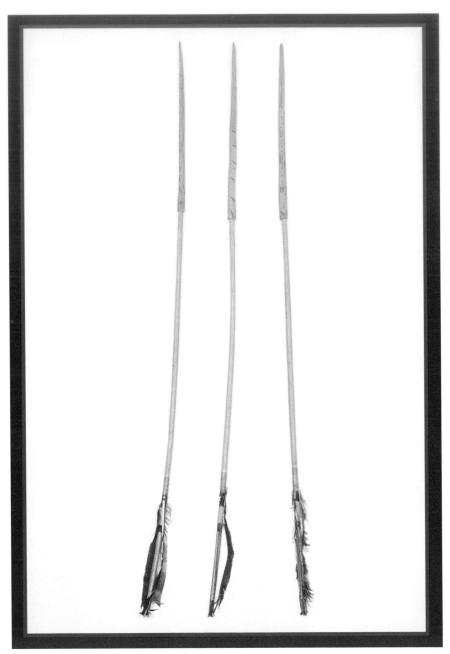

12 Kiowa gaming arrows such as these were thrown by hand. They were similar to the javelin. The player who threw it the farthest won.

animals. The fresh meat and skins were loaded on travois attached to horses and returned to the group's camp. This way of life was known as the Plains Indian culture.

The Plains Indian culture spread over a wide area. It stretched from the area of present-day provinces of southern Canada, Manitoba, Saskatchewan, and Alberta, to southern Texas. The east to west boundaries were the Mississippi Valley to the Rocky Mountains.

To the east of the Crows lived a confederacy of tribes. A confederacy is a union of tribes with a common purpose. This union had three tribes: the Arikaras, the Hidatsas, and the Mandans. The Arikaras were farmers, but they also hunted buffalo. The Kiowas and the Arikaras became good friends. The Arikaras traded corn and tobacco for Kiowa meat and hides.

Although their friends the Crows and the tribes of the confederacy were settled people, the Kiowas remained nomads within the Black Hills. They made a permanent alliance with the Crows around 1700. An alliance is a friendly agreement to work together. For seventy-five years, the Kiowas called the Black Hills their home. Plains Indian life was lived on horseback. It was a nomadic way of life. The Kiowas had always been nomads so they adapted to Plains culture easily.

Two

Kiowa on the Plains

Everything that the Kiowas owned had to be packed for travel. Before they were introduced to horses, the Kiowas used dogs harnessed to travois to carry their possessions. In their new way of life, the Kiowas harnessed the travois to horses. The poles of the horse travois were longer. The longer poles could support a bigger net or platform strapped between the poles for carrying bundles. The poles used for the travois were also used as the foundation poles for the Kiowas' shelters.

The Kiowa shelters were tepees. Tepees were cone-shaped tents. They were supported by twenty or more poles tied together at the top and spread in a circle at the base. A cover made from tanned buffalo hides was stretched around the frame of poles to form a tent. A flap of hide covered the doorway. The flaps on Kiowa tepees were very large compared to those of other tribes who lived in tepees. This marked the Kiowa tepees as different. Sometimes the Kiowa referred to themselves as *Kom-pa-bianta*, "people of the large tepee flaps."

Every part of the buffalo that the Kiowa hunted was put to good use. The hide was used for tepee covers, robes, moccasins, and containers. Strips of braided rawhide were used to make rope. Sinew, a strong fiber that connects muscle to bone, was used as thread. Bones

This photo shows a Kiowa adult and child setting up a tepee.

were used for scraping tools, needles and awls for sewing, and paint-brushes. The horns from the buffalo were made into cups and spoons.

Food and Cooking

Buffalo were the main source of food and hides for the Kiowas. Buffalo meat was made into pemmican by cutting it into thin strips. It was then pounded and mixed with berries and fat. It also was made into jerky—dried strips of meat. Pemmican and jerky were "trail food." They could be eaten on the move, no cooking required.

Meals served when the Kiowas camped had more variety. Meat might be roasted, boiled, or broiled. Fruits, vegetables, nuts, and leaves were gathered and cooked to add to the meal. Kiowas took grains, beans, corn, and melon in trade with other groups. Bread and cakes were baked in the ashes of the campfires.

Clothing and Body Decoration

The Kiowas used buckskin, or tanned deer hide, to make their clothing. The men wore a strip of wool cloth about a foot wide between their legs and tied to their waist by a buckskin thong. (It is not known what was used as a breechcloth before contact with Europeans.) Their breechcloths hung almost to the ground. Their moccasins had soft buckskin uppers and buffalo rawhide soles.

The flaps were decorated with beads and fringe. Sometimes the Kiowas attached small metal cones to men's moccasin tops, which made tinkling sounds as they walked. Kiowa men wore shirts and leggings made of tanned buckskin and decorated with fringe and beads.

Men wore their hair cut short on the right side to fall even with the bottom of the ear, so that it did not interfere with shooting a bow. The hair was long and braided on the left side. The braids were decorated with leather strips, feathers, and metal or were wrapped in fur. Men wore breastplates of bone. Necklaces of beads, pendants on leather strips, and earrings were all part of a Kiowa man's outfit.

Men and women's clothing were both made from soft, tanned

This Kiowa girl's dress is made of buckskin and decorated with paint and beads.

17

deer and elk skin. It is not known what Kiowa women's clothes looked like before coming to the southern plains and having contact with Europeans. We do know from articles collected and photos that they wore buckskin dresses decorated with elk teeth, fringe, and beads. The women wore knee-high boots decorated with beads, fringe, and nickel silver harness spots. They decorated

their clothing with beads, shell, fringe, paint, and elk teeth. As did the men, women wore necklaces, pendants, and earrings made of beads, shells, and metal. Children wore clothing similar to that of the adults.

Some Kiowa women wore tattoos from designs adapted from their neighbor tribe, the Mandans. The women let their hair grow long to hang down around their shoulders or to be worked into braids.

After coming into contact with Europeans, some Kiowa clothing customs changed while others stayed the same. This studio portrait of Sitting-in-the-Saddle shows him wearing a hair pipe breastplate, scarves in his braids, and a fur turban with a feather in it.

These Kiowa girls are wearing clothing decorated with shell and fringe.

They painted their faces and sometimes parts of their hair with vermilion. Vermilion is a substance made of mercury and sulfur that is used as a red pigment. The Kiowas obtained vermilion in trade with settlers.

Artists of the Plains

The Kiowas did not have a written language. Instead, they painted scenes from their lives on their clothes and tepees. Kiowa history was painted on tanned deer hide, tanned buffalo hide, and later on cloth and paper.

There were three types of hide paintings: calendars, personal records or biographies, and imaginative visions. A man's deeds were recorded in pictures that decorated the walls of his tepee. The inside of his buffalo robe would also show scenes of his war deeds or unusual experiences. The colors came from natural sources such as berries, leaves, and charcoal. When the painting was complete, a thin layer of glue was applied over the paint to set it. This artwork was highly valued.

Kiowa women were skilled artists. They decorated clothing and other personal belongings with geometric designs. Women created designs on clothing using glass beads. Their beadwork was beautiful and highly prized.

This Kiowa dance shield is decorated with green paint, feathers, and a horse tail.

Three

Kiowa Society and Religion

Rank played an important part in Kiowa society. A man could gain or lose rank based on his deeds. Rank could be gained through good deeds and tribal praise. Heroic deeds could be accomplished during war raids. Bad deeds, such as lying, stealing, or killing a member of the group, would cause a man to lose rank.

The group took pride in men's deeds, such as hunting, fighting, or gaining wealth. Women gained status through the achievements of their fathers, husbands, or sons. However, Kiowa women were in charge of everyone and everything in and around the tepee. From the animals that the men hunted, the women made food, clothing, moccasins, bags, and other useful items.

There were four social classes within the Kiowa: Onde, Ondegup'a, Kaan, and Dapom. Top rank in Kiowa society was the Onde. Men of the first rank were great warriors. They owned and watched over the ten medicine bundles. Known as the Ten Grandmothers, these medicine bundles were very important in the Kiowa religion. Onde men were wealthy. Their conduct was that of a gentleman—generous, considerate, and courteous. If they were not, they lost rank. Men and women were born Onde. This rank made up about 10 percent of the tribe.

This portrait of a Kiowa bride and groom was probably taken in the late 1800s or early 1900s.

People who were of the second rank were called Ondegup'a. Men in this rank or class were second best as warriors. These men could also be wealthy, but lacked sufficient skill in war to obtain the first rank. This group represented 40 percent of the Kiowas.

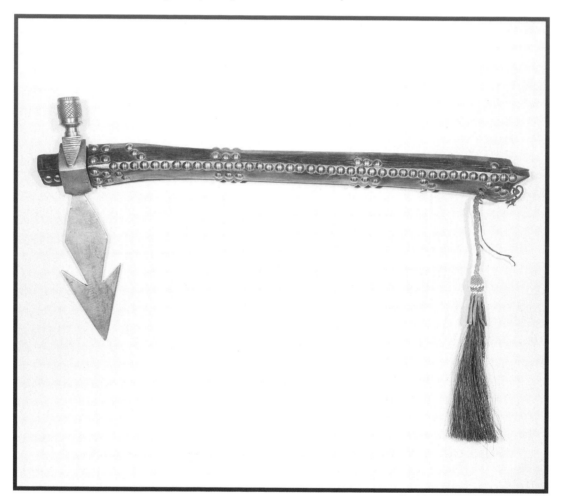

This photo shows a Kiowa pipe tomahawk.

The poor people of the tribe were the Kaan. These people were ranked third and made up about fifty percent of the Kiowas. At the bottom of the Kiowa social ladder were the Dapom. Few people belonged to this rank. They were the misfits, outcasts, and mentally ill.

War was the best opportunity for a man to rise in rank. A war-raid would be fought to gain horses and wealth, or to take revenge. Deeds done bravely in battle gained a man the title of *kietai*, "warrior." Extremely heroic deeds in battle earned a man the title of *kietaisopan*, "great warrior." A man could rise to the position of chief through his war skills and leadership ability.

The Kiowas were led by a chief, but they were divided into subtribes or bands. Each subtribe had its own chief who was subject to the head tribal chief. The Kiowas had six subtribes or bands, which were:

- Kata, "Biters and Arikaras"
- Kogui, "Elks"
- Kaigwu, "Kiowa Proper"
- Kingep, "Big Shields"
- Semat, "Thieves" or "Kiowa-Apaches"
- Kongtalyui, "Black Boys" or "Sindiyuis"

As did other Plains tribes, the Kiowas had military societies. The societies were ranked by age and achievement. There were six military societies among the Kiowas. They were:

- Polanyup, "Rabbits"
- Adaltoyuo, "Young Sheep"
- Tsentanmo, "Horse Headdresses"
- Tonkonko, "Black Legs"
- Taupeko, "Skunkberry People" or "Crazy Horses"
- Kaitsenko (or Koitsenko), "Real Dogs" or "Principal Dogs"

All of the above military societies were considered Dog Soldiers and would act as camp police. The top ranked society was the Principal Dogs. Membership in this group was reserved for the ten best warriors in the tribe. These men were the leaders at tribal ceremonies. They also acted as camp police and guards during a hunt.

Warrior training began early. Boys from eight to ten years of age were called to perform the Rabbit Dance. This dance allowed them to enter the Rabbit military society. In this society, the boys learned how to be warriors. Based on their skill, the boys moved up through the ranked military societies. Around the age of eight, girls started to learn the ways of the tepee from their mothers and grandmothers.

Men, women, boys, and girls all had their work to do. But life for the Kiowas was not all work. The Kiowas' leisure time was spent in recreation, playing games such as dice. The two sexes played these games separately. Music and pipe smoking were also a part of Kiowa leisure time.

Kiowa Religion

The Kiowas believed that everything in nature had a spirit. Human beings, animals, plants, and rocks had a spirit and a power or magic. Kiowas believed that magic from the natural world could be shared or passed along if the right ritual was performed. The Kiowas did not believe that human beings were superior to other living things. They tried to live in harmony with the natural world.

Kiowas believed that the most powerful spirit with the greatest magic was the sun. They knew the power of the sun before they met the Crows and learned of the Sun Dance medicine. One of their legends tells of the marriage between a Kiowa girl and the sun:

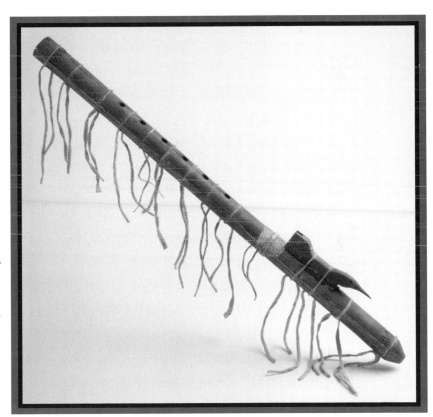

Kiowas played flutes like this one during their leisure time.

The girl found a porcupine in a tree. She climbed the tree to reach the animal. The tree shot up into the heavens and the porcupine changed into a man. She could see he was the sun. They married and had a baby boy.

The sun told his wife never to go near a certain bush. She did not listen. She pulled the bush out of the ground. It made a hole in the heavens. The Kiowa girl could see her people on Earth. She was homesick. She made a rope, put her child on her back, and began to climb down the rope to her people. The sun saw her climbing down the rope. The sun was angry. He threw a stone at her and killed her. Their child fell to Earth with a ring in his hand. Spider Woman found and raised him. She warned the boy never to throw the ring into the sky. The boy disobeyed and threw the ring straight up in the sky. It fell on his head and cut him in half, turning him into twins.

Many Kiowa legends tell of the brave deeds of the Half Boys. The end of the legend says one of the boys walked into a lake and disappeared. The other boy became the medicine in the ten bundles known as the Ten Grandmothers.

These bundles are sacred to the Kiowa and play an important part in their religious ceremonies. In earlier times, each bundle had its own tepee and was watched over by a tribal medicine man. Offerings and prayers were and still are made to these bundles.

When the Kiowas became friends with the Crows, they learned about the Sun Dance. The Sun Dance was the main religious ceremony of the Plains Indian culture. It was held every year in late spring or early summer. All the Kiowas came together to make a great camp. The dance lasted ten days total—six days to prepare and four days to dance.

The Sun Dance was held for several reasons. It strengthened the tribal bonds, and served as a get-together and a time for courtship. It also was used to cure illnesses and to make war medicine so that they would be successful on raids against their enemies.

Other Rituals

Rituals and ceremonies were performed during the lifetime of a Kiowa. Marriage was a simple exchange of gifts. The only birth ritual was the naming of the child, which happened soon after the child was born.

When a Kiowa died, he or she was buried. Because the Kiowas were nomads, a prolonged illness was a problem. The sick or dying were hard to take care of on the move. The old and the sick were often left behind to die when the group moved on. Once a Kiowa died, his or her name was never spoken again.

Taking a sweat bath was often part of Kiowa religious rituals. A man would enter a small lodge in which there were heated rocks placed in a pit in the center. He would pray and burn cedar incense.

Water would be poured over the heated rocks, creating steam vapor. The hot steam would cause the man to sweat. After hours in the lodge, the man would rush into the nearest lake or river. The sweat bath made the body pure for the religious ceremony. A sweat lodge was also used to cure the sick.

Dancing played a part in many Kiowa religious ceremonies. Pipe smoking, prayers, and the sacrifice of valued possessions were also a part of their religious rituals.

When a young man was ready to prove himself as a warrior, he sought power or magic from the natural world. He undertook a vision quest to gain a guardian spirit. Taking no food with him, a young man left his camp to find a lonely spot. There he prayed and waited for a sign or vision. The spirit that spoke to him during this time would be his guide in all things. A man's spirit guide would instruct him in what songs to sing and how to paint himself before battle. This spirit would also guide him in religious rituals.

Dancing was part of Kiowa religious rituals.

Stories in the Sky

The Kiowas have used stories of gods, heroes, and supernatural beings to keep track of their history and their place on Earth. The hero stories tell of warriors facing big challenges, usually large animals. The heroic adventures are played out on Earth, but the stories of gods and supernatural beings are played out in the sky.

The sky stories tell how the Kiowas began and help to explain natural wonders. One of the sky stories, "The Seven Sisters," is about the Kiowas and the stars.

One day, eight children were at play. One of the children was a boy. Suddenly, the boy could not speak. He fell down and began to run around on his hands and feet. He trembled and shook. His skin became fur and his nails became claws. His sisters were terrified. Their brother had turned into a large bear. The bear charged them. It was clear he wanted to eat them. The girls ran and the bear followed them. The girls came to the stump of a great tree. The tree spoke to them. The stump told the girls to climb up on it. When all seven girls were on the stump, it began to rise into the air. The bear came after them but they were just out of reach. The bear clawed at the tree stump. The tree stump kept rising. Finally, the stump threw the sisters into the sky where they became the seven stars of the Big Dipper. It is said as long as the legend lives and the Seven Sisters shine, the Kiowa have kinsmen in the sky and will survive.

The Seven Sisters story is reassuring. It says that no matter how much trouble comes their way, the Kiowas will survive. The story also places the Kiowas in the Black Hills around a rock formation referred to today as the Devil's Tower. This mountain-high rock formation is found in the northeast corner of Wyoming. The rock looks as if it had been clawed by a bear.

The Devil's Tower in Wyoming is the inspiration for Kiowa stories. 33

Four

Contact and Conflict

The Kiowa were already living in the Black Hills when the French began to explore the Missouri River. The French explorer La Salle (René-Robert Cavelier, Sieur de La Salle) had explored the Mississippi and claimed all the territory it drained for France. He built a fort near present-day St. Louis and one where the big river drained into the Gulf of Mexico. He was on his way back to Canada when he heard about the Kiowas from a Pani Indian boy held captive at Fort St. Louis. La Salle mentioned the Kiowas in a diary entry dated some time in 1682. He called them "Manrhoats."

The Kiowas were mentioned by the famous explorers Meriwether Lewis and William Clark in their expedition diaries. The explorers did not see the Kiowas, but heard about them from the Mandans in 1804. Zebulon M. Pike, the explorer for whom Pikes Peak is named, came in contact with the Kiowas. In 1807, he met a group of Kiowas and Comanches returning from a trading expedition with the Mandans. The Kiowas traded fur with the European and United States explorers and traders. They traded for guns and other metal goods.

Contact with these people brought diseases to the Kiowas. Diseases such as smallpox killed many Indians living in the

René-Robert Cavelier, Sieur de La Salle was the first European explorer to hear of the Kiowa.

36 This photo shows a Comanche warrior. When Europeans introduced guns to Native Americans, conflicts became more deadly.

Black Hills. The guns helped the Kiowas become better hunters. The diseases, however, weakened them and reduced the tribal population. The Kiowas had always been a small tribe. They could not afford to lose many people. Their safety depended on strong warriors for hunting and protection from their enemies.

Kiowa and Their Neighbors

Some Native American groups also posed a threat to the Kiowas. The Comanches lived south of the Kiowas. Comanche warriors were great horsemen. They roamed from the Black Hills down into Mexico. The Kiowas called them Gyai'ko, or "enemies." Comanches were also nomadic hunters who depended on the buffalo for their daily needs.

The Dakota Sioux were enemies of the Kiowas. The Dakotas were fierce warriors, and they outnumbered the Kiowas. The Dakotas warred with the Kiowas and the Comanches. Conflict with the powerful Dakotas drove the two tribes south into the southern plains around 1775.

The Kiowas lost one of their bands in the conflict with the Dakotas. The chief of the Kuato band urged his people to stay and fight. They held out for five years until the Dakotas killed them all.

On the southern plains, the Kiowas and Comanches roamed from Oklahoma across Texas to New Mexico. This time, however, the Kiowas ruled. They began to push the Comanches further south.

Peace

Around 1790, a trader in New Mexico arranged for a Kiowa chief, Kooy-skaw-day, "Wolf Lying Down," and the Comanche leader, Pareiya, "Afraid-Of-Water," to discuss peace. Wolf Lying Down agreed to go to the Comanche camp on a fork of the Brazos River in Texas. The other Kiowa were told to go away, but to return when the leaves turned yellow. If Wolf Lying Down was not there, his people were told to avenge his death. The Kiowa chief spent a pleasant summer with the Comanches. When fall arrived, the Kiowas and Comanches made peace. They also made an agreement to help each other in war and peace.

This alliance took over the southern Great Plains. Their territory ran between the Arkansas and Red Rivers, and from Oklahoma through Texas into New Mexico. Together, the Kiowas and Comanches pushed other Native American groups out of the territory. The Kiowas and Comanches raided as far south as Mexico and west to the Gulf of California. They also raided north into Colorado.

The Kiowas and Comanches still hunted the buffalo for necessities, such as food and clothes. The raiding parties, however, were undertaken to gain wealth, such as horses, and captives to be turned into slaves.

The star cluster known as the Seven Sisters is found in the constellation that we know as the Big Dipper.

The Kiowa and Comanche leaders were able to make peace near the
Brazos River in Texas.

Between the Kiowas and Comanches, the Kiowas were the stronger group. They had a reputation as fierce fighters. Many Native American groups found it wise to make peace with the Kiowas rather than to fight them. The Kiowas, along with their friends the Comanches, became rulers of the southern plains. Those who resisted their authority suffered. The Cheyenne and the Osage continued to resist until 1834. That year most of the Kiowa's enemies made peace with them.

Trials in Texas

Although Native Americans accepted the Kiowas' rule of the plains, the settlers did not. People from the United States had been pouring into Spanish territory, modern-day northern Mexico and Texas, in search of land and opportunity. The settlers built homes and towns. They fenced large sections of grassland, and they viewed the buffalo as pests. The settlers shot hundreds of the animals and left them to rot on the plains. The U.S. government encouraged people to kill buffalo. The government knew that without the buffalo, the Indians would be forced to give up their fight and live on a reservation, or else face starvation.

The Kiowas could not understand why buffalo were being massacred. They only killed enough buffalo for their needs. They thought what the settlers did was wasteful. It was also a threat to

Kiowa warriors became rulers of the southern plains along with the Comanches.

the Kiowa way of life. To stop the buffalo slaughter, the Kiowas attacked the settlers.

These attacks caused the settlers to fear the Kiowas. The people in what is now Texas organized a military group to guard their settlements. This military group later became the Texas Rangers.

The Kiowas continued their raids into the northern part of Texas. The Texans were busy in the southern part of the state. They were fighting for independence from Mexico. The Texans declared themselves independent in 1836. Texas joined the United States in 1845 and turned their "Indian problem" over to the U.S. military.

The clash between the Kiowas and the settlers continued. In 1848, gold was discovered in California. The rush of settlers traveling across Kiowa territory increased. This increased contact also brought another disease: cholera. This dangerous disease of the intestines killed more than half of the Kiowas. The Kiowas took revenge by raiding and killing settlers who tried to cross the southern Great Plains. The Kiowa revenge delayed western settlement for forty years.

With the help of the U.S. military, Texas responded to the increased raids by building a string of forts. This line of forts ran from Fort Graham near Austin up to Fort Worth. The forts did not help. They were spaced too far apart. Indian raiding parties could slip by them with ease.

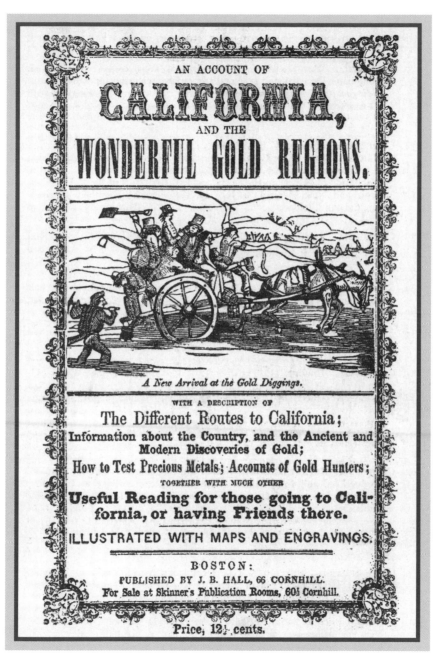

The California Gold Rush of 1849 increased the number of settlers crossing Kiowa territory.

44 Horseback, a Native American Noconee Comanche chief, was among those who signed the Medicine Lodge Treaty in 1867. In the Medicine Lodge Treaty, the Kiowas agreed to settle on a reservation.

The U.S. government tried to stop the raids by asking the Native Americans to sign peace treaties. Between the 1830s and 1860s a number of treaties were signed between the U.S. government and the Plains Indian groups. In the Medicine Lodge Treaty, signed in 1867, the Kiowas agreed to settle on a reservation south of the Arkansas River in western Oklahoma and the Texas panhandle.

Although the Kiowas had signed a treaty to settle on a reservation, they did not remain on it. They continued their raids on the settlers in Texas. Two things happened to contribute to the troubles in Texas. First, the state had withdrawn from the United States to join the Confederacy during the Civil War (1861–1865). Then the U.S. military left Texas. Texas once again had to deal with the Indians. The Texas Rangers took up the job.

Texas's withdrawal led the Native Americans to think of the United States and Texas as two different nations. The Kiowas' Chief Dohasan thought he was making peace with the United States, not the Texans. The Kiowas thought that Texas was a different country and that the agreements with the United States did not apply to Texans. Also, Chief Dohasan died in 1866. Lone Wolf took his place. Lone Wolf could not control the young warriors. Rank could not be achieved by staying on the reservation.

On May 19, 1871, the lone survivor of a wagon train massacred by the Kiowas at Salt Creek staggered into Fort Richardson, near Jacksboro, Texas. William Tecumseh Sherman, commanding general of the U.S. Army, heard the man's report. Sherman was at Fort Richardson on his annual inspection tour. General Sherman ordered the arrest of the Kiowa chiefs involved. Chiefs Satanta, Satank, and Big Tree were taken prisoner in Oklahoma and sent back to Texas.

Satank was a noted leader of the Principal Dogs, the highest-ranked Kiowa military society. The members of this society vowed to return from battle with honor or die trying. On the way back to Texas, Satank died trying. He attacked his military guards and was shot dead.

Satanta and Big Tree stood trial for murder. It is reported that Satanta and Big Tree were the first Native Americans put on trial by a white man's court. The two chiefs were found guilty and sentenced to death. The judge, on a request from the U.S. government, changed the sentences to life in prison. Texas governor Edmund J. Davis also bowed to the government's request and paroled the chiefs in 1873.

Kiowa raids in Texas began again. Satanta was arrested again and sent back to prison in Huntsville, Texas. Big Tree fled. Big Tree was caught, paroled, and pardoned. He returned to the reservation and received a land allotment and lived in Mountain View for the remainder of his life.

Satanta could not stand the confinement of prison. Known as the best speaker among the Plains Indians, he was called the Orator of the Plains. He once said, "When I roam over the

This sculpture of Satanta, also known as White Bear, is on display at the National Hall of Fame for American Indians in Anadarko, Oklahoma.

By the late 1800s, Plains Indian life was coming to an end. This portrait of Comanche Lena was probably taken during the period in which Plains Indians were living on reservations.

prairie I feel free and happy, but when I sit down I grow pale and die." Rather than sit in prison, Satanta committed suicide.

The war between Texas and the Kiowas came to an end after the death of Satanta. The tribe was forced onto a reservation in Oklahoma. Their horses were killed in battle and the buffalo were being killed by settlers. The Plains Indian life was finished.

Five
Adapting and Thriving

Life on the reservation was very hard on the Kiowas. They had been wanderers for as long as any could remember. They counted their status by the distance that they could see. On the open prairie, they had freedom to travel. On the reservation, they had to settle on one piece of land. But the Kiowa have always been smart, adaptable people. Some of the old war chiefs saw that education would be the way to survive. They encouraged their people to send their children to school, but the Kiowa needed more than book learning to change from Plains Indian culture to European-style culture.

On the reservation, some of the old ways of life still existed. The Kiowas lived in tents of canvas. They cooked over open fires. The military societies were reorganized into reservation police forces. By the end of the nineteenth century, however, there was great pressure to open the reservation to white settlement. The Jerome Act of 1892 did away with the reservation. Each Native American was given a piece of land. The rest of the reservation land was opened to sale for the public.

Now the Kiowa had to live in houses and cook on iron stoves. They had to learn how to make clothing from cloth rather than

These Kiowa girls watch respectfully as adults dance during the Tonkonga, the Kiowa Black Leggings Ritual Powwow.

leather. Most members of the tribe could adapt to the new ways. Others had more difficulty.

In 1924, all Native Americans were declared citizens of the United States. But citizenship did not bring equality for the Kiowas and other Native American nations. The U.S. government policy had been to discourage the Indians from speaking their native language, or practicing their religious beliefs and other cultural activities.

The Kiowa Five, pictured here with Oscar Brousse Jacobson of the University of Oklahoma, became celebrities when they attended the university and became part of the international art world.

Kiowa Artists

Artists of the plains became better known after the wars on the southern Great Plains ended. The last skirmish occurred in 1878. A group of seventy-two Kiowa, Arapaho, and Cheyenne warriors were sent to prison in Florida to insure their tribes' good behavior. The warriors were given an education and the opportunity to draw. These artists produced a distinctive style. Their work is exhibited at the Smithsonian Institute in Washington, D.C.

Another group of Kiowa artists became well known in the early part of the twentieth century. They helped to develop the Oklahoma school of art. The most famous are the Kiowa Five—Spencer Asah, James Auchiah, Jack Hokeah, Stephen Mopope, and Monroe Tsatoke. For a short period, the group included Lois Smokey. They all studied at the University of Oklahoma in the 1920s. Samples of these artists' works can also be found at the Smithsonian.

Painting and craftwork are not the only art skills that the Kiowas possess. Many share their cultural experience through music, dance, and writing. Perhaps the best known Kiowa writer is N. Scott Momaday. A poet, nonfiction writer, and novelist, Momaday won the Pulitzer Prize in fiction for his story *House Made of Dawn*. The story was based on the lives of his ancestors.

Reforms finally came under Harold Ickes, secretary of the interior for President Franklin Roosevelt. He was appointed in 1933, and his department included the Office of Indian Affairs. During his tenure, the Indian Reorganization Act of 1934 gave Native Americans the chance for self-government. It gave them the chance to become business owners through government loans. It gave them the right to keep their own ethnic and social traditions and language and still become part of American society.

In the 1950s, a part of Kiowa culture was revived. The old military societies were reorganized into ceremonial dance societies. These societies recreate the old war dances and compete against other Indian groups in annual powwows. Powwows are Indian Cultural Heritage fairs. Today a line of Kiowa dancers dressed in traditional costume might include a lawyer, a welder, a dentist, or a professional model.

The Kiowa Tribal Council was organized in 1968. The Council oversees tribal affairs. The Kiowa Housing Authority helps tribe members find better housing. The Indian Religious Freedom Act of 1994 allowed the Kiowas and other Native Americans the chance to return to some of their earlier religious practices, which had been banned.

There are about 11,500 enrolled members of the Kiowa tribe and the list is growing. Look up in the night sky! The Seven Sisters still live in the Big Dipper. The Kiowas still have kinsmen in the heavens. The Kiowas have survived.

Timeline

Prehistory	Kiowas lived and hunted in the mountains of what is now southeast British Columbia. They moved south into present-day Yellowstone National Park.
1682	French explorer La Salle learns about Manrhoats (Kiowas) from a Pani Indian boy held captive at Fort St. Louis. The Kiowas were then living in the Black Hills.
Around 1700	Kiowas make an enduring alliance with the Crow Indians.
1775	Dakotas push the Kiowas and Comanches out of the Black Hills.
1790	Kiowas and Comanches make a lasting peace and an alliance to help each other.
1804	The Lewis and Clark expedition diaries note hearing about the Kiowas.
1807	Zebulon M. Pike, explorer for whom Pikes Peak is named, meets the Kiowas.

1834	Most southwestern Great Plains Indian tribes make peace with the Kiowas.
1836	Texas declares independence from Mexico and organizes a military group to fight the Kiowas.
1848	Gold is discovered in California. In 1849, U.S. citizens rush to the gold fields across Kiowa territory.
1861–1865	Texas leaves the United States and joins the Confederate States during the Civil War. Texas' separation from the United States leads Kiowas to think the treaties with the United States do not apply to Texas.
1867	Kiowas sign the Medicine Lodge treaty with the United States. In it, they agree to settle on a reservation in southern Oklahoma.
1866	The great Kiowa chief Dohasan dies. Lone Wolf becomes chief.
1871	Kiowas massacre a wagon train of traders at Salt Creek in northern Texas. General William Tecumseh Sherman, commanding general of the U.S. Army, orders the Kiowa chiefs involved in the massacre arrested. Chiefs Satank, Satanta, and Big Tree are arrested, tried, and sentenced to die.

1873	Governor Edmund J. Davis of Texas, on request from the U.S. government, paroles the Kiowa chiefs.
1887	The last Sun Dance is performed. The United States halts the Kiowa religious ritual.
1892	The Jerome Act eliminates reservations in Oklahoma. Each Kiowa person is given a piece of land.
1924	The U.S. government makes all Native Americans citizens.
1934	The Indian Reorganization Act gives Native Americans more rights to self-government, and to obtain government loans for business and reestablish their cultural heritage.
1950s	Kiowa military societies are reestablished as ceremonial dance societies.
1968	Kiowa Tribal Council is organized.

Glossary and Pronunciation Guide

alliance (uh-LY-uhns)   A friendly agreement to work together.

cholera (KAH-luh-ruh)   A dangerous disease of the intestines.

epidemic (eh-puh-DEH-mik)   An epidemic happens when an infectious disease spreads quickly through a group of people.

Kiowa (KEE-uh-wuh)   A Plains Indian Tribe that roamed over Oklahoma, Texas, and New Mexico.

nomad (NOH-mad)   A member of a tribe that wanders around instead of living in one place.

pipestone (PYP-stohn)   A claylike stone the Indians used to make smoking pipes.

travois (TRA-vwah)   Carrying device made of two poles attached by a harness to a pack animal. A net, animal skin, or wood platform is attached to the two poles. Supplies are tied on to this platform.

vermilion (ver-MIL-yuhn)   A red pigment made of mercury and sulfur.

Resources

BOOKS

Marriott, Alice. *The Ten Grandmothers*. Norman, OK: University of Oklahoma Press, 1983.

Mayhall, Mildred P. *The Kiowas*. Norman, OK: University of Oklahoma Press, 1984.

Meadows, William C. *Kiowa, Apache, and Comanche Military Societies: Enduring Veterans, 1800 to the Present*. Austin, TX: University of Texas Press, 1999.

Momaday, N. (Natachee) Scott. *The Way to Rainy Mountain*. Albuquerque, New Mexico: University of New Mexico Press, 2001.

Newcomb, Jr., W. W. *The Indians of Texas, From Prehistoric to Modern Times*. Austin, TX: University of Texas Press, 1985.

Nye, Wilbur Sturtevant. *Bad Medicine & Good*. Norman, OK: University of Oklahoma Press, 1997.

Wright, Muriel H. *A Guide to the Indian Tribes of Oklahoma*. Norman, OK: University of Oklahoma Press, 1987.

ORGANIZATIONS

Kiowa Tribal Museum
Box 369
Carnegie, OK 73015
(580) 654-2300

Oklahoma Historical Society
2100 North Lincoln Boulevard
Oklahoma City, OK 73015
(405) 521-2491
Web site: http://www.ok-history.mus.ok.us

Panhandle-Plains Historical Museum
2503 Fourth Avenue, Unit 60967
Canyon, TX 79015
(806) 651-2244
Web site: http://www.panhandleplains.org

Sam Noble Oklahoma Museum of Natural History
2401 Chautauqua Avenue
Norman, OK 73072
(405) 325-4712
Web site: http://www.snomnh.ou.edu

WEB SITES

Due to the changing nature of Internet links, PowerKids Press has developed an online list of Web sites related to the subject of this book. This site is updated regularly. Please use this link to access the site:

www.powerkidslinks.com/lna/kiowa

Index